GAYLORD NELSON

A Day for the Earth

GAYLORD NELSON

A Day for the Earth

Jeffrey Shulman and Teresa Rogers
Illustrated by Larry Raymond

Twenty-First Century Books

A Division of Henry Holt and Co., Inc.

Frederick, Maryland

Published by
Twenty-First Century Books
A Division of Henry Holt and Co., Inc.
38 South Market Street
Frederick, Maryland 21701

Text Copyright © 1992
Twenty-First Century Books

Illustrations Copyright © 1992
Twenty-First Century Books

Printed in the United States of America

10 9 8 7 6 5 4 3 2 1

Library of Congress Cataloging in Publication Data

Shulman, Jeffrey
Gaylord Nelson: A Day for the Earth
Illustrated by Larry Raymond

(An Earth Keepers Book)
Includes glossary and index.
Summary: Examines the life and work of the politician who worked
on the state and national level to protect the environment and was
responsible for the first Earth Day in 1970.
1. Nelson, Gaylord, 1916- —Juvenile literature.
2. Legislators—United States—Biography—Juvenile literature.
3. Environmentalists—United States—Biography—Juvenile literature.
4. Conservationists—United States—Biography—Juvenile literature.
5. Governors—Wisconsin—Biography—Juvenile literature.
6. United States. Congress. Senate—Biography—Juvenile literature.
[1. Nelson, Gaylord, 1916- . 2. Legislators. 3. Conservationists.]
I. Rogers, Teresa. II. Raymond, Larry, ill. III. Title. IV. Series: Earth Keepers
E748.N43S48 1991
328.73'092—dc20 [B] 91-19777 CIP AC
ISBN 0-941477-40-1

CONTENTS

Chapter 1

A New Way of Thinking

From his seat on the stage, Gaylord Nelson watched the crowd gather before him. The capitol building was in the distance. Its tall spire was shrouded by the shadows of the April clouds.

Gaylord Nelson knew that building well. He spent 10 years there as a state senator serving the people of Dane County, Wisconsin. And he was often at the capitol building during the four years he served as governor of the state. During those years, he worked to pass laws that would improve the lives of the people of Wisconsin.

As he watched the shadows cover the capitol building, Nelson thought for a moment about other places he knew well. His mind wandered off to the wilderness areas of northern Wisconsin—to the shores of the Apostle Islands, to the banks of the St. Croix River. As governor, Gaylord Nelson had fought to conserve, or save, these and other wilderness areas. In fact, he had worked so hard to conserve the natural resources of Wisconsin, to keep them safe and clean for future use, that he earned the name, "Wisconsin's conservation governor."

Now Nelson was representing the people of Wisconsin in the U.S. Senate. He had come home to speak about the environment. In his 22 years of public service, Gaylord Nelson had made hundreds of such speeches—about the need to preserve the country's natural resources, about the dangers of pollution, and about endangered species of plants and animals.

But as spring shadows began to cast their darkness, the senator knew that his speech this evening marked a special occasion.

It was April 21, 1970, and tomorrow was Earth Day, the first national day of activities to teach people about the environmental dangers that faced the earth. Earth Day was Senator Nelson's idea. Six months before, Nelson had stood up in the Senate of the United States to call for "a national teach-in on the crisis of the environment."

Senator Nelson wanted the entire nation to set aside one day a year "to present the facts about our environment clearly and dramatically."

That day was scheduled for April 22, 1970.

Gaylord Nelson was glad to be in Wisconsin on the evening before Earth Day. This was the place and these were the people he knew best. He was born here—in Clear Lake, Wisconsin, a small town in the northwestern part of the state. He would never forget the woods and streams, the lakes and marshes, of his boyhood home.

It was there that Gaylord Nelson formed a lifelong love of nature and a deep belief that the natural world belongs to all people. It was there that a young Gaylord Nelson became convinced that it was government's job to serve the people and protect their world.

When it was his turn to speak, Nelson shrugged off the tired feeling brought on by a day of making speeches. "Earth Day can be a turning point in American history," he read, slowly and softly.

Gaylord Nelson looked at the crowd before him on the University of Wisconsin campus. Wherever he spoke about the environment, young people were the first to listen to him.

As he watched the faces of these students, he knew that the future of the earth rested with them, with a new generation of people determined to save the natural world. As always, he seemed to gather strength from the young and hopeful faces of his audience.

"Earth Day can be the birth date of a new way of thinking," Nelson continued, "a way of thinking that says, 'This land was not put here for us to use up.' Earth Day can be the beginning of a way of thinking that says, 'Even a country as rich as ours must depend on the natural systems that preserve the air, the water, and the land.'"

Nelson's voice grew stronger and more determined. Gaylord Nelson is known as a soft-spoken and friendly man, relaxed and funny. He is an easy person to like, and one who easily likes others. But when he gets angry, a friend of his once said, "he can give a speech that sends goose pimples up and down your spine."

"Our society cannot survive," he told his audience, "if we spoil the land and water. We cannot survive if we spoil the air." He talked about the balance of nature and about the slow and careful way that nature changes over time. He talked about the harmful changes made to the environment by careless and thoughtless people.

"The future can be preserved only if *we* change," he continued, "only if we change our attitudes toward nature and nature's works. Winning the environmental war is tougher by far than winning any other war. It will take a commitment far beyond any effort ever made before."

Nelson leaned toward his audience. "Are we able to do this?" he asked. "Yes!" he answered confidently.

"But are we *willing* to do this?" he asked. He paused and studied the thoughtful faces of his audience. "That is the unanswered question."

As Gaylord Nelson walked back to his seat, he wasn't listening to the applause of the crowd. His attention was already on the next day—on Earth Day, 1970.

*"There was a special adventure to being
a young boy in northwestern Wisconsin."*

Chapter 2

The Special Adventure

"You can take most boys out of the country," said a friend of Gaylord Nelson. "But in Gaylord's case, he just took Clear Lake with him."

Gaylord Anton Nelson was born in the small town of Clear Lake, Wisconsin, on June 4, 1916. Nestled in the lake-dotted countryside of northwestern Wisconsin, Clear Lake was a town of 700 people. Main Street was only three blocks long.

Where Main Street stopped, the Wisconsin wilderness began. The marsh at the end of Main Street, overgrown with cattails and lily pads, was home to muskrats and nesting birds. Nearby were the clear and cold waters of the many lakes created by the glaciers that moved across this area 10,000 years ago.

Beyond the edge of town was forestland that stretched north to Lake Superior and the Minnesota border.

"There was a special adventure to being a young boy in northwestern Wisconsin," Gaylord Nelson later wrote. "There was the adventure of exploring a deep green pine forest, crunching noisily through the crisp leaves and pine needles on a sharp fall day, or taking a cool drink from a fast running trout stream or a hidden lake."

Long after he left Clear Lake, Gaylord Nelson kept with him this memory of his hometown. "He took his love of nature with him," one of his friends said, "and turned it into remarkable environmental legislation."

For a young boy growing up in Clear Lake, it seemed that the whole world shared the special adventure of being close to nature. "There was never any reason to believe that the rest of the world wasn't as clean and comfortable as northern Wisconsin," Gaylord later recalled. "It was easy for the children of Clear Lake to believe that the legacy they had inherited in rich land, clean air, and safe water was one every boy and girl in the nation had."

Nicknamed "Happy," Gaylord was the third of four children born to Anton and Mary Nelson. His sister Janet was four years older, and Peg was two years older. His brother, Stan, was two years younger to the day, born on June 4, 1918.

"It isn't fair," Gaylord used to complain. "We only get one birthday party."

"Clear Lake was an ideal place to grow up," Gaylord observed many years later. "It was the kind of community where everyone knew everyone else, where everyone was concerned about everyone else."

Everyone in the community knew Gaylord's parents. Anton Nelson was the town's doctor, serving the people of the Wisconsin countryside for miles around. Gaylord's mother, Mary Bradt Nelson, was a nurse and the head of the Polk County Red Cross Committee. Mary Nelson, like her husband, was also actively involved in town affairs and politics.

"Very intelligent" is how Gaylord Nelson remembers his parents. Anton Nelson graduated first in his class from medical school, and Mary Nelson was first in her nursing-school class. Both Anton and Mary Nelson encouraged an early love of reading, and Gaylord Nelson recalls a household full of books and magazines.

"Do you want to be a doctor?" Gaylord's father would ask him. "Yes!" was Gaylord's reply as he watched his father work. Young Gaylord had a chance to find out what being a country doctor was like. He often went with his father to visit the outlying farms when someone was sick.

If the roads were covered with snow, Gaylord and his father would wrap themselves in their coonskin coats and harness the horses to the sleigh. Covered by a big, bearskin blanket, they talked about the world outside Clear Lake. To Gaylord, it seemed that his father knew all the answers. On their way home, riding under the bright Wisconsin stars, Gaylord and his father would nestle down beneath the bearskin blanket to sleep. The horses knew the way back to the barn.

The Nelson family enjoyed high-school football and basketball games as well as Saturday evening concerts at the town bandstand. At night, the Nelsons would read or listen to radio programs. There were Sunday afternoon rides in the new automobile, a 1923 Model-T Ford.

The nickname "Happy" was a fitting one for young Gaylord Nelson. He was happiest when he was outdoors. Gaylord was often out fishing or looking for frogs by the marshy shore of Mud Lake. In summertime, Gaylord and his friends swam in the nearby rivers. They skated on the frozen lakes during the long Wisconsin winters.

Such outdoor activities kept the boys of Clear Lake busy. In fact, when Gaylord once visited the big city of St. Paul, Minnesota, he found that he quickly grew bored. "I just couldn't figure out what city kids did for fun," he later recalled.

Gaylord Nelson was an active boy—and sometimes a mischievous one. On summer days, Gaylord could often be found snaring gophers in the fields nearby. Gaylord knew how to imitate the whistling sound that gophers make. He and his friends would quietly creep through the grass and place a string trap inside one of the gopher holes. "You'd whistle," Gaylord recalled years later, "and they'd stick their heads up—and you got 'em!"

One time, Gaylord and his boyhood friend Sherman Benson caught about 10 gophers this way. They led the gophers, tied together on a string, to Gaylord's back yard, where they put them in a cage. But the gophers managed to dig out from under the cage, and they were soon all over town. "There were gophers in everybody's yard that summer!" Gaylord Nelson remembers.

Snaring gophers was not the only form of mischief for Clear Lake boys. Gaylord and Sherman also enjoyed trying to confuse the Mud Lake turtles.

"Every fall, just like clockwork," Gaylord recalls, "all the turtles in Little Clear Lake and Big Clear Lake would head across the town to Mud Lake. They were going to hibernate there for the winter. And they all started on the same day. Now the town was between the lakes. So the turtles would come up through the village—a parade of

turtles down Main Street. They would cross the yards and streets. Everyone in Clear Lake would look out for them."

Gaylord and his friend Sherman would try to bewilder the turtles. "We'd pick them up and put them behind trees or buildings. We'd turn them around, facing the way they came. But as soon as they stuck their heads out, they would turn back around and march on to Mud Lake. I couldn't understand how they could find their way. And, you know, I'm still wondering how they could do it."

As he grew up, Gaylord developed interests besides snaring gophers and confusing Mud Lake turtles. He was active in sports and was the captain of his high-school basketball and football teams. He also played the trumpet in the high-school band. Gaylord continued to read as much as he could. "Everything I could get my hands on," he says. "That's what I read."

He also became interested in politics. The Nelsons had a long history of service to the community, and politics was often the talk around the dinner table. Anton Nelson served as mayor of Clear Lake, and Gaylord's mother was a member of several important political committees.

Both Anton and Mary Nelson were active supporters of "Fighting" Bob La Follette and his Progressive Party. La Follette was a politician who thought that government should be more concerned about helping people. His party wanted to change laws to make them more fair to working and poor people. Too often, La Follette argued, politicians only listened to the men who ran big businesses.

As Gaylord Nelson listened to his family's discussions, he decided that he didn't want to be a doctor. He wanted to be a politician, the kind of leader who helped people. He wanted to be like "Fighting" Bob La Follette.

Whenever a Progressive Party speaker was near Clear Lake, the Nelsons would, according to Gaylord, "jump in the Model-T, and away we'd go." On one such occasion, when Gaylord was 10 years old, he sat on his father's shoulders to hear Bob La Follette speak. La Follette stood on the rear platform of a train and delivered a rousing speech to the biggest crowd Gaylord had ever seen.

"Would you rather be a politician when you grow up?" Gaylord's father asked him on the way home.

"Yes, I would," Gaylord answered, "but I'm afraid that Bob La Follette will solve all the problems and there won't be anything left for me to do."

"We ought to leave some of nature's work unimproved by the hand of man."

Chapter 3

The Governor from Clear Lake

Gaylord Nelson knew he wanted to be a politician. But the road to the Governor's Mansion took a number of unexpected twists and turns.

Gaylord got his first taste of Wisconsin politics when he was 14. He went before the town council to urge the planting of elm trees on the five roads that led into Clear Lake. Gaylord could imagine the shady, green canopy that the trees would provide in later years. The council members politely listened to his request and just as politely chose to ignore it.

This was Gaylord Nelson's first political fight—and he lost. It was an early start to his political career, and it would not be his last defeat. Gaylord Nelson learned at an early age that losing was a part of politics.

Gaylord graduated from Clear Lake High School in 1934. He went on to attend San Jose State College in San

Jose, California, the school his sister Janet had attended before him. After his graduation in 1939, he entered the University of Wisconsin Law School. He received his law degree in 1942.

Nelson served in the U.S. Army for almost four years, as World War II raged across Europe and Asia. But the most important part of his military career, he says, was meeting a pretty Army nurse by the name of Carrie Lee Dotson. They would be married soon after the war.

By 1946, Nelson was back in Wisconsin—and back in politics. He ran for a seat in the state assembly from Polk County, the county where Clear Lake is located. But his second try at Wisconsin politics was no more successful than his first. Gaylord Nelson lost the election. It was close, however. He lost by only a hundred votes.

In 1947, Gaylord and Carrie Lee were married. They moved to Madison, Wisconsin, the state capital, where Nelson practiced law for two years. Their first home was a small apartment tucked between an Italian restaurant and a vacuum cleaner repair shop.

The political "bug" had bitten Nelson, and he was ready for another try at winning a public office. In 1948, he ran for the Wisconsin state senate as a member of the Democratic Party, and this time he won. He would be re-elected to this position in 1952 and 1956, holding the senate seat for 10 years.

During these years, Nelson's influence as a politician grew. In the state senate, he served on committees dealing with such matters as public education and conservation. For many years, Nelson was the leader of the Wisconsin Democratic Party.

Nelson's political influence was not the only thing that was growing during these years. He and Carrie Lee had a growing family to take care of, too. Gaylord Anton, Jr., (also nicknamed "Happy") was born in 1953. Three years later, Cynthia Lee (called "Tia") joined the family. A third child, Jeffrey Andrew, was born in 1961.

The Nelsons moved to a big, old house on a quiet, oak-lined street in Crestwood, a suburb of Madison. Their household was a busy one. The Nelson home was always alive with the sound of children playing games or neighbors stopping by to visit.

There was also the sound of adults discussing politics. Nelson and his friends often argued about current issues and events. They discussed past elections and the future of the Wisconsin Democratic Party.

In the early months of 1958, these late-night political discussions grew even longer and louder. Gaylord Nelson had decided to run for governor on the Democratic ticket. He and his supporters knew that it would be a tough political fight. Wisconsin was a strong Republican state. There hadn't been a Democratic governor of Wisconsin since 1932.

Soon into the political campaign, Nelson suffered a great personal loss. His father had a stroke the same night

Nelson was chosen by the Democratic Party to run for governor. Gaylord Nelson rushed to the hospital to be by his father's side.

His father looked at Gaylord, a grown man now, but he remembered a young boy sitting on his shoulders to catch a glimpse of a visiting politician. Looking at his son, Anton Nelson asked, "Well, do you think Bob La Follette left enough problems for you?" Gaylord Nelson's father died two weeks later.

It was a hard-fought campaign, and Nelson was away from his family most of the time. But when the votes were counted on November 4, 1958, Gaylord, Jr., and Tia Nelson had a new home. Their father had been elected governor of Wisconsin, and the Nelson family was moving to the Governor's Mansion.

"Wow!" cried young Gaylord, Jr., as he stared at the huge rooms of the mansion. It didn't take long, however, for the children to make themselves at home. They enjoyed playing hide-and-seek in the mansion's 20 rooms. They might even greet one of the Nelsons' guests by sliding down the long, curving banister that led to the central hallway. "After all," explained Wisconsin's new governor, "they can't wear the place down any more than the 5,000 visitors we have every year."

Carrie Lee and Gaylord Nelson settled easily into their new home, too. The Governor's Mansion was a welcome spot for the numerous guests who came to visit or work. Once again, the talk around the Nelson household was politics. It was not unusual, Carrie Lee remembers, to find Gaylord and his friends "talking and arguing far into the night about politics and government."

If a break was needed from politics, Nelson would tell one of his "Clear Lake stories." He quickly became known for his funny tales of youthful adventures with his boyhood friends. Nelson always joined the laughter, especially when the joke was on him.

When he wasn't preparing for meetings or reading committee reports, Nelson might be found in the kitchen preparing his special Chinese meatball soup. But Carrie Lee had learned not to expect her husband to be much help around the house. She said that Gaylord couldn't "tell the difference between a hammer and a screwdriver."

Governor Nelson was respected for his honesty and friendliness. Nelson was said to have a "kindly, direct charm." He was a warm and outgoing man, even with his political opponents. "In many ways, he's never outgrown Clear Lake," said one friend, "where he knew and liked everybody."

There were other ways that Gaylord Nelson had never outgrown Clear Lake. He never forgot "the rich land, the clean air, and the safe water" that, he said, every boy and girl enjoyed there. As governor, Nelson wanted everyone in Wisconsin to have that kind of environment.

Nelson's interest in the environment was influenced by the writings of Aldo Leopold. Leopold was a former employee of the U.S. Forest Service and, from 1933 to his death in 1948, a professor of wildlife management at the University of Wisconsin. His best-known book, *A Sand County Almanac* (published after his death) describes the beauty of the natural world and calls for a "land ethic" to protect and preserve wilderness areas.

To Nelson, Aldo Leopold knew the world of nature better than anyone else who had written on the subject. "It was his idea that we ought to leave some of nature's work unimproved by the hand of man," Nelson said. "He understood that people need to be alone with nature."

Once in office, Governor Nelson worked to put that idea into action. Re-reading *A Sand County Almanac*, he looked for ways to preserve more of Wisconsin's lakes and rivers, wetlands and marshes. "I wish Leopold was still alive," Nelson said. "I'd put him in a job where he could do something."

But the environment was not the only problem facing Wisconsin and its new governor. Like "Fighting" Bob La Follette, Gaylord Nelson wanted government to listen to and help the people of his state. Nelson worked to pass laws that would improve education, the health care of elderly people, and automobile safety. He supported laws that protected the rights of women, minorities, children, and the disabled. He created new divisions in the state government so that public officials could respond more quickly to the needs of the people.

It was not until 1961, after he had been re-elected as governor, that Gaylord Nelson really had the opportunity to do something about the environment. Then, he began a 10-year, $50 million program to buy privately owned lands and to preserve them as wilderness areas.

Under this new program, the state of Wisconsin saved hundreds of thousands of acres for recreation areas, public parks, and wildlife habitats. These areas now belonged to the people of Wisconsin. They would remain untouched by progress and development—no housing, no highways, no shopping centers—forever.

"They were places where people would always be able to enjoy clean air and water," Nelson said, "where people could escape the crowded cities and enjoy the beauty and peace of nature."

To Gaylord Nelson, this kind of program preserved more than natural resources and scenic areas. It preserved the way of life he had known in Clear Lake.

It was a program for Wisconsin's future. And for the rest of his career, Nelson would consider this preservation program as one of his proudest accomplishments.

As governor, Nelson also took a strong stand against pollution. When he learned that laundry detergents were polluting the water supply, Nelson set up a committee to study the problem. The committee's report led to new laws that made Wisconsin the first state in the nation to regulate the use of such detergent products. During this time, Wisconsin also adopted strict laws against littering and dumping trash.

When he was elected governor of Wisconsin in 1958, Gaylord Nelson said that he wanted to make the state "a proud pioneer for a better life." The years ahead would prove that he had succeeded. Wisconsin's environmental program became a model for similar plans in other states.

"As far as the environment goes," Nelson later wrote, "Wisconsin was a seedbed for new ideas and approaches." Under the leadership of the governor from Clear Lake, the state of Wisconsin did, in fact, become a pioneer in environmental protection.

36

Chapter 4

Senator Nelson

In 1962, after two terms as governor of Wisconsin, Gaylord Nelson was elected to represent the people of Wisconsin in the U.S. Senate.

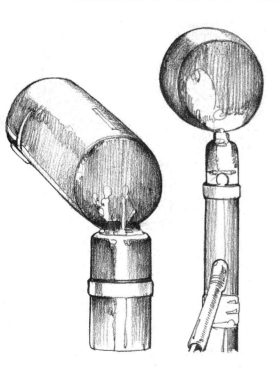

Nelson had made the environment an important part of his campaign. It wasn't enough, he said, for the states to protect and preserve their natural resources. The crisis of the environment, he argued, was far too big a problem for the states to handle by themselves.

Nelson believed that the federal government had to become involved. He decided to fight for the future of the earth at the national level.

On the morning of March 25, 1963, Gaylord Nelson prepared to make a speech on the environment. He had spoken about the problems facing the country's natural resources many times before, but never to so important an audience. This time, he was standing on the floor of the Senate of the United States. He was about to make his first speech as a senator from the state of Wisconsin.

Nelson began by describing the preservation program he had developed for the state of Wisconsin. But that effort was not enough, he insisted. "We need a comprehensive and nationwide program to save the natural resources of America," he argued.

"We cannot be blind," he said to the other senators, "to the growing crisis of our environment. Our soil, our water, and our air are becoming more polluted every day. Our most priceless natural resources—trees, lakes, rivers, wildlife habitats, scenic landscapes—are being destroyed."

When he rose to speak that March morning, Gaylord Nelson was one of very few politicians talking about the environment. It was simply not an issue that many other political leaders were concerned about.

"When I arrived as a senator from Wisconsin in 1963," Nelson later wrote, "there were probably only 20 members of Congress, out of 535, who would have considered themselves to be environmentalists. In fact, even in the 1968 presidential campaign, not a single environmental speech was given by a presidential candidate."

Other politicians asked the new senator from Wisconsin why he insisted on talking about such an unpopular issue. "Because people care," Nelson responded. "People care about the disappearance of their favorite childhood nature spots."

As a senator, Gaylord Nelson spoke out for what he believed. Throughout his political career, Nelson took a clear stand on tough issues. Whether the issue was health care or education, highway safety or energy policy, Nelson was not afraid to take an unpopular position.

"You have to stand up when you think you're right," Gaylord Nelson stated. In 1965, when President Lyndon Johnson wanted money to send more soldiers to fight the Vietnam War, Senator Nelson had to make one of the most unpopular decisions of his political career. He was one of only three U.S. senators to vote against the president. "I need my conscience," he said, "more than the president needs my vote."

On many issues, Nelson did not stand alone for long. More often than not, his positions came to be seen as the right ones. By the time he left the U.S. Senate in 1980, for instance, politicians everywhere were speaking about the earth and environmental issues.

But it wasn't enough, Nelson believed, just to make speeches about the environment. He wanted to take action. He wanted to see change. He had learned as a boy that government should make a difference in people's lives. He had seen that lesson at work first as a state senator and then as governor. Nelson had come to believe that everyone had a right to a clean and safe environment. Now, as a U.S. senator, Nelson was determined to pass new laws that would protect the earth.

In his 18 years as a U.S. senator, Nelson worked on hundreds of such laws. The first proposal he introduced in the Senate was similar to a law he had developed as the governor of Wisconsin. It was designed to prevent water pollution caused by the use of laundry detergents. But he soon learned that creating new legislation at the national level is a difficult and time-consuming process.

The process of making new laws involves working closely with different groups. Senator Nelson listened to the detergent producers, to environmental activists, and to homemakers who use detergent products. Each of these groups had its own point of view, and Nelson had to think about their concerns when he wrote his new law.

It took a year for the Senate to pass Nelson's proposal to control detergents. The Senate then sent the measure to the House of Representatives for its approval. But the House never approved the idea.

This was not the first time Gaylord Nelson had lost a fight on behalf of the environment. But, as before, he was not going to give up. "We must continue to fight the destruction of our natural environment," he said.

To Nelson, the fight for the environment meant laws to stop pollution, laws to preserve wilderness areas, and laws to educate the American people about the growing environmental crisis. The battle to save the earth, he wrote, was "America's last chance."

As he spent more time on these issues, Nelson looked to the future for the answers to environmental problems. He felt that the nation's best hope for a new beginning rested with its young people. The future of the earth, he thought, was in their hands.

With this idea in mind, Nelson turned his attention to educating people about the environment. He wanted the fate of the earth to be everyone's concern. As part of this effort, Nelson persuaded President John F. Kennedy to undertake a national tour in support of the environment in 1963.

Kennedy's first stop was a visit to northern Wisconsin. Nelson wanted President Kennedy to see firsthand the value of preserving wilderness areas. "What has been done here," the president said, "must be done in every state in the country."

Nelson knew, however, that the future of the earth depended on more than politicians and laws. It depended on people and their attitudes. Protecting the environment meant changing the way people think about their daily lives. It meant understanding "that human activities have created an environmental crisis," Nelson said.

Changing people's attitudes toward the environment was on Senator Nelson's mind when, in the summer of 1969, he attended a meeting on water pollution in Santa Barbara, California. The previous January, Santa Barbara had been the scene of a massive oil spill.

The beaches had been covered with a thick layer of black muck. Sea birds struggled for life, and dead fish washed up on shore. The sandy Santa Barbara coastline had not fully recovered when Nelson visited that August.

On the plane ride out of Santa Barbara, Nelson read a story about students who thought that the Vietnam War was wrong. These students decided to hold a series of programs designed to teach people about the war. Called teach-ins, these programs combined speeches, classes, and other activities.

"Suddenly, the idea occurred to me: Why not have a teach-in on the environment? That's how the idea for Earth Day was born."

When Nelson got back to Washington, he announced his idea on the floor of the U.S. Senate. "The youth of today face an ugly world of the future with dangerously and deadly polluted air and water," he began his speech. "I am proposing a national teach-in on the crisis of the environment."

It wasn't long before Senator Gaylord Nelson knew he had started something big. "The phone was just ringing off the hook," he recalls.

Chapter 5

Earth Day

The response to Senator Nelson's call for a national teach-in on the environment was overwhelming.

"The idea took off," he said. "I was getting calls from people all over the country asking what they could do. I got calls from 90 senators asking for my speeches. They had never given an environmental speech before."

Nelson set up a small staff, headed by a student named Denis Hayes, to plan the event. Hayes contacted about 400 colleges to help with Earth Day activities. But 1,600 other colleges developed programs on their own. So did over 10,000 public and private schools. In communities across the nation, people set aside April 22, 1970, as a day to celebrate the earth.

"The reason Earth Day worked," Nelson says, "is that it organized itself. The idea was out there, and everybody grabbed it!"

Over 20 million Americans grabbed the idea. That's how many took part in the day's events. "I was looking for a demonstration so big that the politicians would have to pay attention," Nelson said. "I wanted a demonstration by so many people that politicians would say, 'Holy Cow, people care about this.' That's just what Earth Day did."

In New York City, school children got out of bed at dawn to clean up dirty city streets. High-school students washed the windows of subway cars. Community groups planted trees and shrubs in city parks.

Busy Manhattan streets were closed to cars and buses. Over 100,000 people walked up and down the streets in a nonpolluting parade. Some people found more inventive means of getting around: bikes, pogo sticks, and roller skates were among the favorite forms of transportation.

Across the country, protests called "trash-ins" brought attention to waste and garbage. In West Virginia, students picked up five tons of trash along a short stretch of highway and then dumped the garbage on the steps of the county courthouse. On the polluted Potomac River near Washington, D.C., Girl Scouts used canoes to dredge up piles of junk. High-school students in Omaha, Nebraska, made a tin mountain from the beer and soft-drink cans they had collected—over 156,000 of them!

EARTH DAY
1970

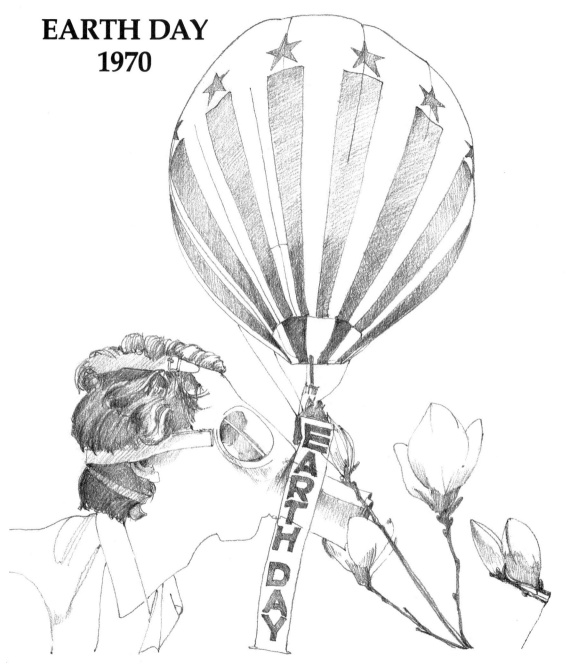

EARTH DAY

People everywhere took to the streets to show how they felt. In Tacoma, Washington, 100 high-school students rode down a city highway on horseback to demonstrate against gas fumes from cars and buses. Marchers began a 500-mile "Survival Walk" along the freeways of southern California. City council members in Buffalo, New York, called for a community clean-up campaign by parading through the town with brooms and shovels.

People wore gas masks to protest air pollution. They decorated trees with garbage picked up from city streets. In Albuquerque, New Mexico, politicians who had voted against tough environmental laws were given "Enemy of the Earth" awards. Students in New Orleans, Louisiana, named the oil industry as "Polluter of the Month."

"It's nothing short of incredible," said Nelson as he surveyed the crowds in city after city. "The people cared," the senator was pleased to report. "And they sent a big message to the politicians—a message to tell them to wake up and do something."

"Nothing like this has ever happened before," Senator Nelson noted.

For millions of Americans, April 22, 1970, was a day devoted to a better earth. For Nelson, it was also a weary day of traveling and speechmaking.

But this time, the voices of many other politicians were heard, too. Mayors, governors, and more than 500 members of Congress joined what Senator Hugh Scott called "the mighty voice" of the environmental movement.

In New Jersey, Michigan, Massachusetts, Maryland, Ohio, and other states, lawmakers observed Earth Day by passing new regulations to protect the environment. As the *New York Times* reported, "It seemed that everyone was for Earth Day."

Wherever he went, Nelson spoke to young people. In the spirit of America's youth, he said, was "our only hope for saving the environment and putting quality back into life." Wherever he went, he felt that spirit and saw that sense of hope.

"Across America, there is a disgust, a rising anger, a demand for action," Nelson said. "Earth Day demonstrates the widespread concern for a livable world. It makes me believe for the first time that we can wage a successful fight to save the earth."

Nelson asked his listeners to think of themselves not just as citizens of the United States, but as citizens of the earth. He called this idea "environmental citizenship." He asked his listeners to think not just of themselves, but of their children and their children's children.

At stop after stop, Nelson sounded a call to action. Speeches and demonstrations are not enough, he insisted. "We need action. We need political action nationwide to restore the quality of our environment. Americans must start now to take a stand."

According to some reports, Earth Day, 1970 was the biggest demonstration in America's history. It proved, said Nelson, that millions of Americans *were* ready to take a stand for the environment. They were ready to join the fight for a cleaner and safer world.

Gaylord Nelson, the founder of Earth Day, knew that the fight ahead would not be an easy one.

"It could be one of the toughest fights this country has ever seen," he warned.

Chapter 6

A Mighty Voice

As Gaylord Nelson hoped, Earth Day was a turning point in American history. There would be many tough fights ahead. But after April 22, 1970, politicians could no longer choose to ignore "the mighty voice" of the environmental movement.

Once the public had spoken out in such a dramatic way, Nelson wrote, "the question was no longer *whether* environmental change would come—it was a question of *how* it would come."

Change came with tougher laws. In the years after Earth Day, the U.S. Congress and many state governments passed new laws to keep the environment clean and safe, to protect animals in danger of becoming extinct, and to create public parks, national forests, and wildlife refuges. And new government agencies, such as the Environmental Protection Agency, were set up to make sure that people followed these laws.

"Earth Day achieved what I had in mind," Nelson remarked. "It set the stage for new laws, and that was important. The environment became, for the first time, part of American politics."

From 1970 to 1980, Senator Nelson worked with other political leaders to pass tough, new environmental laws. Nelson fought to control the use of chemical pesticides by introducing the National Pesticide Control Act. The Water Quality Act, sponsored by Nelson, called for an end to the pollution of the world's oceans. The Clean Air Act set new and stricter national standards for the quality of our air.

Nelson had been one of the first major public figures to speak out against pollution. Now he worked to protect rivers and lakes from the factories that were dumping poisonous wastes. The National Lakes Preservation Act, introduced by Nelson, began a new program to restore endangered waterways.

Nelson was eager to preserve wilderness areas across America, from the marshlands of northern Wisconsin to the snow-covered passes of the Colorado mountains. He sought to protect both the hillsides of West Virginia and the Atlantic Ocean shoreline from mining operations. His Wild Rivers Act saved some of America's unspoiled rivers.

He developed The National Hiking Trails System, a nationwide system of hiking trails protected by the federal government. Nelson found that there was "tremendous political support" for the idea of preserving these wilderness routes. The success of this proposal, he said, "was a case of the right person being at the right location at just the right time."

Included in this system is the Appalachian Trail, which runs for 2,000 miles from Maine to Georgia. The Pacific

Crest Trail, a protected route that follows the high ridges of the western mountain ranges, winds from Canada to Mexico. In Gaylord Nelson's home state, the Ice Age Trail wanders along the rugged glacial landscape of northern Wisconsin for hundreds of miles.

Despite these successes, Gaylord Nelson was defeated when he ran for a fourth Senate term in 1980. He had been a senator for 18 years. His defeat that November surprised his supporters and saddened many people. But Nelson had learned long ago that losing is part of politics.

"Being a senator was the job I always wanted to do," he said at the time. "I've loved every minute of it. I thought about it when I was a little boy, and I'd like to continue. But I can't. When you're licked, you're licked. This is no job for crybabies."

"From the day you're elected," Gaylord Nelson said, "you have to keep in mind that one day somebody's going to beat you."

In the weeks ahead, Nelson would have the painful tasks of saying good-bye to his staff and cleaning out his office. There were tears shed among his many friends, but not by Gaylord. "Gaylord just takes things in stride," says Carrie Lee Nelson.

It was the end of a remarkable political career.

Gaylord Nelson enjoyed that career. "It was a wonderful era," he says, "and I had a wonderful time." But he also says that he wouldn't go back. He has more time now to spend with Carrie Lee, more time to visit with his two grandchildren, Kiva and Jason. "It's a real treat for

Gaylord to be with young children," observes Carrie Lee, "to see how they act and to watch them grow." It's a treat for the children to be with their "Poppa," too.

Gaylord Nelson's defeat, however, was not the end of his environmental career.

After his loss in 1980, Nelson went to work for The Wilderness Society, a private group that tries to protect the natural condition of public land. Aldo Leopold, whose writings inspired Wisconsin's conservation governor, was one of the founders of The Wilderness Society.

"Environmental issues are more important than ever," Nelson says. "So here I am."

Today, Nelson sees himself as carrying on the work of Leopold and many others who devoted their lives to protecting the earth. Nelson's hair is a little thinner and his glasses a little thicker than they were when he gave his first speech as a senator. But his passion to preserve the quality of the environment is just as strong.

"My main interest for 32 years in public office," he says, "was the issue of the environment. But we still have to deal with powerful forces in this country who do not believe the problem is serious."

Nelson continues to keep politicians informed about the environment. He believes as strongly as ever that "the environment needs to be front-page news."

"It is time for our political leaders to recognize this truth: the fate of the living planet is the most important issue facing mankind," he says. "No other issue, now and for all the centuries to come, is more important to our way of life than the status of our resources—air, water, soil, minerals, scenic beauty, wildlife habitats, rivers, lakes, forests, and oceans."

Chapter 7

The Unanswered Question

For his years of service to the earth, Gaylord Nelson has received many awards from environmental groups. He has been honored in other ways as well. There is a Gaylord Nelson State Park in Madison, Wisconsin. And back in Clear Lake, the town museum is proud to have a Gaylord Nelson room.

In his years of public service, Gaylord Nelson turned an early love of nature into tough environmental laws. But Nelson never thought that change would come by laws alone. "Even more important," he says, "there has been a change in the public attitude and understanding of environmental issues." More people have become aware of the environment; more people have become involved in activities to protect natural resources. "We have come a long way," Nelson points out, "and much more quickly than I thought possible."

In 1967, the word "recycle" was almost unknown. It didn't even appear in most American dictionaries. Now there are recycling programs in thousands of communities.

Today, people are working to save energy. They are concerned about such issues as acid rain, marine and air pollution, and toxic waste. They are worried about the fate of the rain forests and endangered species. According to Gaylord Nelson, this new awareness of environmental problems is the most rewarding tribute to Earth Day.

The truest sign of Earth Day's success, according to Nelson, is that people everywhere are taking a stand on behalf of the environment. This was never clearer than on April 22, 1990, the twentieth anniversary of Earth Day. More than 55 million Americans in 3,600 communities came out to show their support for the earth.

But Earth Day, 1990 was not just an American event. It was a day of protest and concern for people on every continent. From Kenya to Brazil, from Scotland to Belize, more than 200 million people in over 140 countries made it clear that the environment is now a global issue.

The official motto for Earth Day, 1990 was "Think Globally . . . Act Locally." It meant that individuals, working in their own cities and towns, could make a worldwide difference. It meant that improving the environment had

to start with a personal commitment. There were speeches and parades and activities, just as there were 20 years before. One banner seemed to sum up the hopeful and determined mood of the event: "Every Day is Earth Day!"

And just as he was 20 years before, Gaylord Nelson was there. Nelson was Honorary Chairman of Earth Day, 1990. He spoke before huge crowds, urging them to leave a clean and rich and beautiful earth for future generations to enjoy.

"Unless we change our ways," he said, "our legacy will be one of pollution, poverty, and ugliness."

As always, he called on people to take action. When we destroy our earth, Nelson said, "we are stealing from our children, our grandchildren, our great-grandchildren, and future generations. The test of our conscience is our willingness to sacrifice something today for the future. This is a test we now must take—and pass."

As always, he called on young people to take the lead. He asked the leaders of tomorrow to become the "conservation generation." Nelson called Earth Day, 1990 "the last best chance for saving the planet."

He knew the future of the earth was in the hands of a new generation. He knew they would have to make a difference. "Don't look to my generation," Nelson told them. "Look to yours."

"You and the generation after you are going to have to do it," Gaylord Nelson said. "And I think you will."

Glossary

acid rain	a form of precipitation (rain, snow, sleet, hail, mist, fog, dew) made acidic by waste gases
conservation	the process by which natural resources are saved, or conserved
Earth Day	a day set aside each year (April 22) to promote awareness of environmental issues
ecology	the study of living things in their environment
endangered species	a species that has so few members that it is in danger of dying out, or becoming extinct
environment	the physical world that surrounds a plant or animal
environmental citizenship	the idea that people should consider themselves citizens of the earth
environmentalist	a person who seeks to protect the natural environment
habitat	the physical surroundings where a living thing makes its home
land ethic	the idea that people should act in a way that helps to protect and preserve the environment
natural resource	a material or product supplied by nature, such as water, air, minerals, or trees

pesticide	a substance, often a strong chemical, used to kill insect pests
pollution	the process by which a natural environment is made unclean and unfit for living things
preservation	the process by which an environment is kept, or preserved, in its natural condition
recreation area	an area, such as a park or playground, set aside for public enjoyment
recycling	the process by which a waste product is made useable
species	a group of similar plants or animals that can produce offspring
toxic waste	waste products that are poisonous or hazardous to the environment
waste	material that is useless or worthless, such as garbage or trash
wilderness area	an area of land or water permanently protected from development
wildlife	animals or plants living in a natural state
wildlife refuge	an area of land or water set aside as a protected home for wildlife

Index